D1386825

I work in a Supermarket

by Clare Oliver

Photography by Chris Fairclough

FRANKLIN WATTS
LONDON • SYDNEY

This edition 2004

Franklin Watts
96 Leonard Street
London
EC2A 4XD

Franklin Watts Australia
45-51 Huntley Street
Alexandria
NSW 2015

Copyright © 2001 Franklin Watts

Editor: Kate Banham
Designer: Joelle Wheelwright
Art Direction: Jason Anscomb
Photography: Chris Fairclough
Consultant: Beverley Mathias, REACH
REACH is the National Advice Centre for Children with Reading
Difficulties. REACH can be contacted at California Country Park,
Nine Mile Ride, Finchampstead, Berkshire RG40 4HT. Email
them at **reach@reach-reading.demon.co.uk.**

Acknowledgements
The publishers would like to thank Lindsey Benham and the staff
and customers of the Tesco superstore in Bedworth, for their help
in the production of this book.

A CIP catalogue reference for this book is available from the
British Library.

Dewey Decimal Classification 381

ISBN: 0 7496 5637 9

Printed in Malaysia

Contents

(Note: words printed in **bold italics** are explained in the glossary.)

Meet Lindsey

Do you like being busy and helpful? Lindsey does. She has worked as a Customer Assistant in her local Tesco superstore for the last six years. Before that, she worked in another shop – and before that, she was training to be a nurse.

The main part of Lindsey's job is helping the customers with their shopping. She starts work at 8.30 a.m. and goes home at 5 p.m. Her working week is from Tuesday to Saturday, which means that her 'weekend' is on Sunday and Monday. Some staff have to work Sundays, but everyone has two days off like Lindsey does.

◀ This is the supermarket where Lindsey works.

▲ Lindsey helps customers by carrying their shopping.

Lindsey reports to her Section Managers, Jackie and Saffron, but she can also ask for advice from the **Personnel Manager**, Paula.

Lindsey gets on well with her Section Manager, Jackie. ▶

Busy mums have their hands full and can't pack their shopping. That's where Lindsey can help. ▲

Customer Services Assistant

Lindsey's most important duties are:

- Packing bags
- Helping customers who are in wheelchairs
- Helping busy mums or dads
- Showing people where to find things in the store
- Checking barcodes
- Bringing new carrier bags and till rolls to the *cashiers*
- Filling the sweet displays next to the tills

JUST THE JOB!

The Superstore

The supermarket where Lindsey works is a busy place. Lindsey knows it inside-out, because her job involves a lot of running around, to check on prices for example. Also, like most of the staff, she spent some time in each part of the store during her month of initial training.

> Lindsey sometimes has to go and find a product on the shelves. She uses her portable *barcode reader* to find out its price.

After her training, Lindsey worked in the Home and Wear department for about two years. This part of the shop sells clothes, toys and lots of household things.

> When she worked in Home and Wear, Lindsey sorted the clothes by size and colour.

Lindsey joined Customer Services four years ago. Customer Services has its own counter, where staff help customers exchange goods or check a receipt. Most of the time, though, Lindsey stands near the tills – ready to pack shopping.

It's handy having an in-store pharmacy. Lindsey can pick up her mum's *prescription*.

In the tiny room behind the pharmacy, there are drawers of pills and medicine.

Pharmacist

JUST THE JOB!

Paul is a chemist. He works in the in-store pharmacy. He studied Chemistry at university for three years, then did another year of specialist training to get his certificate to *dispense* drugs.

His job includes:
- Advising customers about remedies
- Preparing prescriptions
- Measuring out medicines
- Ordering new stock

Customer service is all about helping people – with a smile. Lindsey knows many of the regular customers, and some people ask specially for her. Sometimes customers ask Lindsey to get items that they can't reach.

Allan can't reach the top shelves, so Lindsey helps him.

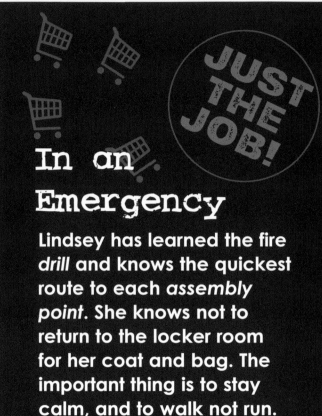

JUST THE JOB!

In an Emergency

Lindsey has learned the fire *drill* and knows the quickest route to each *assembly point*. She knows not to return to the locker room for her coat and bag. The important thing is to stay calm, and to walk not run.

As well as packing bags, Lindsey sometimes goes with people to their car or to the bus-stop. One customer is terrified of lifts, so she usually climbs the stairs to the car park. Lindsey takes the customer's shopping in the lift and meets her at the top!

Shoppers with young children know they can trust Lindsey, too. She will keep an eye on their bags or child while they go to the toilet or change a baby's nappy.

Lindsey minds baby Amy, while mum uses the customer toilet.

Ruth is a regular customer. Lindsey always helps her to unload her trolley into her car.

Top Tips

People can be fussy about how their shopping is packed. Here are Lindsey's top tips:

- Place all the chilled or frozen products together, so they keep each other cold.
- Put anything *fragile* – such as eggs or tomatoes – on the top.
- Cushion bottles and jars with softer items, such as sponges or bags of rice.
- Don't put too many heavy items in one carrier bag – otherwise it might split.

Warehouse Work

Sometimes Lindsey has to go to the warehouse. Maybe a customer has asked for something that they have run out of on the shop floor. Perhaps the cashiers need some new till rolls or carrier bags. Or maybe she just has to print out a new price sign to slip on to a shelf.

> The warehouse is enormous! It may look like chaos, but you soon get to know where everything is.

The warehouse is in the part of the store that customers cannot enter. Lindsey knows where the cashiers' supplies are, because this is the area she goes to most often. She's also got a good idea of where most other things are, even though it seemed like a jumble when she first started.

> The area for cashiers' supplies has till rolls, magazines and boxes of carrier bags.

Many goods are stored on rollcages like this one.

Next to the warehouse is a little office with computers. This is where Lindsey goes to print new price labels and signs.

Lindsey prints a price label for some teabags.

Jobspeak

Lindsey learned some new words when she started working at the store:

Dolly – a little plastic platform with rollers, used for wheeling heavy loads

Pallet – a wooden tray for stacking goods that has slats so it can be lifted with a forklift truck

Rollcage – a metal cage on wheels, with sides but no top, used for moving stacks of boxes

WIGIG – this stands for 'When It's Gone, It's Gone'. It means an item that will only be on sale for a limited time, usually at a special bargain price.

Dinnertime

Lindsey goes to the staff canteen for her lunch and tea breaks. Here, the food is **subsidised**, which means that staff can buy a three-course meal for £1.25. There are also sandwiches and salads for people who don't feel like eating a large meal.

In the staff canteen, Lindsey can tuck into a cheap, delicious lunch.

Favourite Five

Lindsey's favourite lunches are:
- Chicken and chips
- Roast beef and Yorkshire pudding
- Spaghetti bolognaise
- Jacket potato with cheese and salad
- Lasagne

Like all the staff, Lindsey uses a locker to store her belongings safely.

Rather than using cash, Lindsey has a staff card, called a 'cardinal card'. She pays money into a special machine from time to time, and then uses the card to buy things from the canteen.

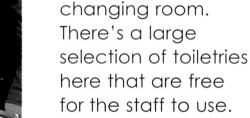
▲ Lindsey tops up her cardinal card with money.

Lindsey makes sure she looks tidy before she goes back to the shop floor. ▲

After lunch, Lindsey freshens up in the changing room. There's a large selection of toiletries here that are free for the staff to use.

Canteen Cook

The canteen cook isn't just busy at lunchtime! Her duties include:
- 'Shopping' in the store for ingredients
- Cooking and serving breakfasts, lunches and dinners
- Making sandwiches
- Taking payment from the workers' cardinal cards
- Writing and putting up menus
- Loading the dishwasher
- Keeping the kitchen spotlessly clean

JUST THE JOB!

Tasty Treats

All the supermarket staff must be able to advise customers about the items on sale. The assistants who work on the delicatessen counter allow customers to taste things before they buy, but there are also tasting sessions for the staff.

When a new product is introduced, there are samples for everyone to try. This is one of Lindsey's favourite **perks** of the job!

Sandra knows how to cut just the right amount of Cheddar.

Amanda lets Lindsey try a cube of a new type of cheese.

Delicatessen Assistant

The staff on the delicatessen counter are taught to:

- Estimate how much items weigh
- Use the cheese slicers safely
- Use the meat slicers safely
- Keep cooked and uncooked meats separate

They also learn how to *tare*. When customers buy products such as hummus that are sold by weight, taring stops them paying for the weight of the tub as well as the food. The staff put an empty tub on the scales first and press a button to cancel out its weight.

Lindsey also does her own shopping in the store. She sometimes buys a snack from Chris on the hot chicken counter, to eat on her way home. As well as chicken, there are also ribs and sausages that are all cooked and ready to eat.

Chris uses a thermometer to check that the chickens are cooked right through.

The delicatessen staff wear plastic gloves to handle the food. They must not allow uncooked meats, such as bacon, to touch cooked meats, such as hams.

We're happy for you to try before you buy

17

The In-store Bakery

One of the busiest areas in the store is the bakery. As well as bread, the bakery makes cookies, muffins, doughnuts and croissants.

To make the bread, all the ingredients are first whizzed up in a huge food mixer. Next, the shaping machine divides the dough into the right-sized pieces.

▲ Carol, the Head Baker, puts the shaped dough into the loaf tins.

The pieces of dough are placed in trays, **proved** to make them rise, and then baked. Finally, the bread is wrapped and priced – once it has cooled a little.

◄ Terry takes some bread rolls out of the proving oven. Some bread is left in there to rise overnight.

Lindsey does not usually go into the bakery – unless the shop is quiet and the staff there need her help. Everyone in the bakery has to wear a hat, so that no hairs get into the food. The regular staff have cotton hats, but there are paper ones by the door for visitors.

One of the bakery workers, Linda, shows Lindsey how to bag up the freshly-baked bread. ▶

Baker

JUST THE JOB!

Carol is the Head Baker.
Her duties include:
- **Making the bread**
- *Supervising* the other bakery staff
- **Ordering fresh supplies**
- **Checking that the bakery shelves are well stocked**

Favourite Five

Lindsey's favourite doughnut flavours are:

- **Vanilla custard**
- **Apple**
- **Jam**
- **Chocolate**
- **Bubble gum**

John is a *maintenance* worker at the store. He has to be on hand in case anything breaks – such as the air conditioning, lighting or freezers. John's workshop is packed with tools, and there are lots of instruction *manuals* for all the different machines.

If anything in the store breaks down – even an office fan – John will try to repair it in his workshop. ▼

Maintenance Man

To be a maintenance man like John you have to enjoy fixing things. You need to be responsible and fill your time wisely – even when there is nothing to fix. John spends a lot of time just checking the machines, keeping them oiled and clean so that they run smoothly. He also rereads the manuals to keep everything fresh in his mind. The best step towards a job like John's is an NVQ, for example in Engineering.

JUST THE JOB!

Lindsey goes to see John if any pods get stuck. The pods are little capsules that the cashiers fill with the money-off coupons they get from the customers. The pod should be sucked up and carried through the building along a network of tubes.

Sometimes Lindsey has to help when things go wrong, too. If anything is spilled or broken, she fetches the cleaning trolley. She puts up a cone, warning customers to stay away from that bit of floor while she clears up the mess.

► If a pod gets stuck, Lindsey might have to call John to sort it out.

► Lindsey puts up a warning cone so that no one slips on the spilt milk.

Clean-up Time

The cleaning trolley has cloths, a bucket of soapy water and a dustpan and brush. It's best to brush up any broken glass first – and Lindsey knows to take care that she doesn't cut herself.

In a job like Lindsey's, you deal with customers all the time and get to know the regulars – it's like seeing old friends when they come in. Lindsey also gets on well with the other staff and looks forward to the staff Christmas party each year.

Many of the staff are young like Lindsey. Lindsey enjoys a friendly chat with Helen, one of the cashiers.

Three-year-old Theo is lost. Lindsey will help him to find his mum or dad.

Lindsey's first choice of job when she left school was nursing, but the shift work was too demanding. Working at the supermarket has boosted her confidence, and she likes to know that she is helping people.

Another great thing about Lindsey's job is all the discounts. She gets ten percent off everything she buys in the store – as well as the subsidised canteen meals. She receives private healthcare, and the company pays money into a private *pension* that will build up for when she eventually *retires*. She even gets a Christmas bonus!

Accounts Assistant

Lindsey's wages are paid directly into her bank account. Janice looks after the wages, and she trained for her job by taking an NVQ in Providing Business Services. Janice gives Lindsey a pay slip each month. This tells Lindsey how much money she has received after tax has been taken off. And it keeps count of other things too, such as how many days of paid holiday she has left for that year.

Wages O...

Each month, Janice, the accounts assistant, gives Lindsey a pay slip, to show how much she has earned.

Lindsey is on her feet all day, often carrying heavy shopping, so her job is very tiring. It's also **mentally** exhausting. It can be hard to be polite if a customer is being rude. Sometimes people complain about the way their bags are packed, or about waiting in queues. Whatever happens, Lindsey must stay cool and calm.

At busy times, Lindsey's job is quite stressful, and she is rushed off her feet. When the store is quiet, Lindsey sometimes has to do quite boring jobs, such as collecting the shopping baskets.

In quiet moments, Lindsey wheels stacks of shopping baskets back to the store entrance.

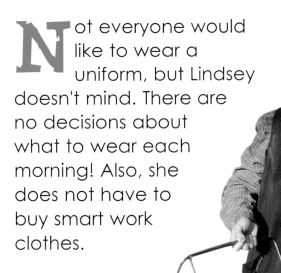

ot everyone would like to wear a uniform, but Lindsey doesn't mind. There are no decisions about what to wear each morning! Also, she does not have to buy smart work clothes.

One of the worst things is having to work on a Saturday. But even that's not so bad. It means that Lindsey is free to go out on a Monday, when places are less crowded.

Essential Kit

Lindsey has a choice of what to wear:
• Dress – checked or patterned
• Navy skirt or trousers
• Blouse – checked or patterned
• Gilet – to keep her warm in winter
Lindsey carries a bleeper in her pocket, so that she knows if a cashier needs her help.

When a customer brings back something they have bought, Lindsey asks them if they would like a replacement or their money back – so long as they have a receipt.

Finding a Job

The only **qualifications** for working in a supermarket are that, like Lindsey, you are polite and hard-working. You have to like people, because you will be dealing with them all day long.

Lindsey does a lot of **voluntary work** for charities such as Help the Aged and the St John's Ambulance. Knowing this, Paula, the Personnel Manager, was sure that Lindsey would be gentle and patient with the customers.

Lindsey knows where most things are in the store – so she's the perfect person to ask if you can't find something!

Lindsey *clocks on* when she starts work and clocks off when she stops. She does this for her lunch and tea breaks too.

Paula checks on Lindsey's progress once a year. She finds out how Lindsey feels about her job and organises any extra training that she might need.

The easiest way to get a supermarket job is to start off doing a Saturday job. Then you can ask the manager if you can have a full-time position when you leave school.

Job Know-How

What qualifications do I need?
None. Supermarket staff are trained on the job.

What personal qualities do I need?
Polite, friendly and reliable. A good memory for remembering where everything is in the store.

How do I apply?
There is probably a noticeboard in your local supermarket, where they advertise if they need workers. You could also speak or write to the store manager.

Will there be an interview?
Yes – to check that you will be able to deal with the customers. But there are many other jobs in a supermarket, too. If you are strong, but like being on your own, you might prefer to work in the warehouse, for example.

Glossary

Assembly point   The place where everyone must go in an emergency.

Barcode reader   A machine that uses a laser to scan the barcode (pattern of black lines) on a product. From this, it can tell details about the product, such as its price.

Cashier   Someone who works on the tills.

Clock on   To record when you arrive at work, by passing a card through a machine that has a clock inside it. When you stop work, you clock off.

Delicatessen   The counter in a supermarket that sells cheese, cooked meats, bacon, salads and dips such as hummus.

Dispense   To prepare and give out medicines.

Drill   The right actions to perform.

Fragile   Easily broken or damaged.

Maintenance   Keeping things (especially machines) in good working order.

Manual   An instruction book.

Mental   To do with the mind.

Pension   Money you receive when you have retired.

Perk   An extra advantage which comes with a job.

Personnel Manager   The person in a company who recruits new staff and is in charge of training existing staff.

Pharmacy   A shop that sells medicines. For some drugs, customers need a prescription from their doctor, but others (such as headache pills and cough medicines) can be bought over the counter.

Prescription   A note from a doctor that tells which medicine a patient needs.

Prove   To make dough rise by keeping it warm.

Qualifications   Official requirements for a particular job.

Retire   To stop working for good, when you get old.

Subsidised   Only having a price that covers part of the cost, with the rest paid by someone else, for example a company.

Supervise   To watch over someone.

Tare   To allow for the weight of a container and subtract it from the overall weight.

Voluntary work   Working for no money, just because you want to help.

Find Out More

This is the supermarket where Lindsey works:

Tesco Superstore
1 Leicester Street
Bedworth
WEST MIDLANDS CV12 8SX

Visit these websites to find out more about supermarkets in the United Kingdom. Many have a page where you can find out about job opportunities:

www.asda.co.uk
www.budgens.co.uk
www.kwiksave.co.uk
www.safeway.co.uk
www.sainsburys.co.uk
www.somerfield.co.uk
www.tesco.com
www.waitrose.com

Find out more about further qualifications by visiting the NVQ website:

www.dfee.gov.uk/nvq

In Australia and New Zealand you can check out:

www.colesonline.com.au or
www.coles.com.au
www.franklins.com.au
www.woolworths.com.au
www.woolworths.co.nz

Or you could try contacting:

Foodtown Supermarkets
(NZ) 09-2752788
Pak N Save Food Warehouses
(NZ) 09-6291600

Also, why don't you...

• Visit your local library and check out the careers section.

• Find out if there is a teacher at your school who is an expert careers advisor.

• Check the noticeboard at your local supermarket to see if there are any vacancies.

• Look in your local business directory under 'Supermarkets' to find out whom to contact for work experience placements.

Index